Original title:
Beneath a Tropical Sky

Copyright © 2025 Creative Arts Management OÜ
All rights reserved.

Author: Levi Montgomery
ISBN HARDBACK: 978-1-80581-648-5
ISBN PAPERBACK: 978-1-80581-175-6
ISBN EBOOK: 978-1-80581-648-5

Whispers of Palms in Gentle Breeze

The palms are gossiping, oh what a scene,
Telling secrets of fish quite obscene.
They sway and they giggle, with a rustle and creak,
As coconuts tumble, their laughter unique.

A parrot named Percy, with flair fits the bill,
Mixin' cocktails with juice, he's a party thrill.
His jokes are like fruits, a bit ripe maybe,
But the fun's in the shade, come laugh with me!

Dance of Shadows on Sandy Shores

The shadows are dancing, doing a jig,
While seagulls join in, looking quite big.
A crab wearing sunglasses, he thinks he's so cool,
Goes side to side, just breaking the rule.

Turtles in flip-flops, parade down the sand,
Waving to tourists, ice cream in hand.
They slip and they slide, making quite a mess,
Who knew a beach trip could bring such distress!

Midnight Serenade by the Ocean's Edge

Under the moonlight, the waves start to play,
With fish on a conga line, splashing away.
A jellyfish DJ spins tunes with great flair,
While sea turtles break dance, without any care.

Crabs are the bouncers, keeping the peace,
While starfish in boas are partying at least.
The seaweed is swaying, with style in its hair,
It's a midnight shindig, all creatures compare!

Sunlit Dreams on Coral Reefs

Coral castles glisten in colors so bright,
With clownfish that giggle, what a silly sight.
A grouper named Gus is the king of the show,
With a crown made of bubbles, watch him steal the glow!

Anemones wink as they sway in the tide,
Whispers of shrimp as they stealthily hide.
A frisky little octopus, drawing a doodle,
Making art in the sand, a true ocean noodle!

A Tapestry of Silhouettes at Twilight

As the sun dips low, shadows play,
Dancing figures on display.
A crab's grand march, a lizard's leap,
In the twilight, secrets creep.

Coconuts roll like bowling balls,
The laughter echoes, nature calls.
A parrot squawks with flair and pride,
As I trip on roots, and glide.

Bananas wearing hats of leaves,
They're the gossipers, I believe!
Chasing fireflies that tease my nose,
In this chaos, wonder grows.

As stars blink in the sky's embrace,
They wink at me, a friendly face.
The night insists I stay awhile,
And join the fun, share a smile.

Golden Hues of Dawn's First Breath

Morning light spills like spilled tea,
Warm and sticky, calls to me.
A rooster crows, a wake-up song,
But I think I'll snooze a bit long.

Mangoes hanging like golden dreams,
Swaying gently on sunlit beams.
A monkey steals my breakfast bowl,
With a grin that steals my soul.

The beach is waking, waves applaud,
As I wrestle with my flip-flop fraud.
Dancing crabs join in the fray,
Who knew they'd steal my shoes today?

With every dawn, a new charade,
Life is crazy, wild parade.
Between the lizards and the cheer,
It's a colorful circus here!

The Heartbeat of a Tropical Sanctuary

Palm trees sway with a giddy grace,
They play the tunes, the sun's embrace.
A squirrel in shades is quite a sight,
Doing yoga, what a delight!

The toucans gossip overhead,
With beaks so bright, they're well-bred.
While iguanas bask and pose,
Like models striking silly throws.

A breeze that tickles, whispers sweet,
Makes even sand feel like a treat.
In this haven, laughter springs,
Oh, what joy this atmosphere brings!

As twilight tugs at the day's end,
With giggles shared, this place we'll send.
To keep the fun beneath the stars,
And dream of humor, near and far.

Tales Told by Flickering Fireflies

Fireflies flicker, what's the scoop?
Like tiny stars that dance and loop.
Their stories twist through humid air,
Of lost socks and other despair.

A meandering frog joins the chat,
With a loud ribbit, "Imagine that!"
Joking about his pond's new glow,
"It's makeup!" he croaks, stealing the show.

Lush green tales of sneaky ants,
Who throw wild parties in their pants.
The moon chuckles, beams from above,
In this quirky land, there's so much love.

As laughter twirls beneath the night,
Every shadow seems to take flight.
Fireflies wink, with mischief they tease,
Under the stars, they bring us glee.

A Portrait of the Islands at Dusk

As the sun dips low, fish start to plot,
A lobster in shades, thinks it's really hot.
The palm trees gossip about the sunsets,
While crabs wear sunglasses, feeling no regrets.

Bamboo slips tequila to a piña colada,
The coconut giggles, what a wild saga!
A breeze plays chess with the sand on the shore,
While the stars pop up, saying, 'We want more!'

Beneath the Gaze of Endless Stars

A parrot tells secrets to a lazy turtle,
While fireflies dance in a bright little circle.
The moon starts to chuckle at the tales spun,
As hammock critters pass around the fun.

Bats wear capes, patrol the night skies,
The owls roll their eyes at the batty flies.
Crickets play music, a symphony sweet,
A conch shell DJ keeps the rhythm neat.

Cascading Rain and Island Joy

Raindrops tap dance on the coconut leaves,
As frogs croak out rhymes, spinning up their eves.
The puddles reflect the shenanigans bold,
While splashy events from the young to the old.

In the midst of showers, a chicken takes flight,
Though wet and confused, it still feels just right.
A duck slides by wearing a waterlogged hat,
With each silly quack, can't quite tell where it's at.

Flickers of Firelight on the Beach

A crab juggles shells under the warm glow,
While tiki torches sway, stealing the show.
The waves come in laughing, tickling the sand,
As flip-flops and laughter go hand in hand.

The marshmallows giggle as they roast with flair,
While the beachball joins in, bouncing in midair.
A toasted coconut starts a conga line,
In the light of the fire, everything's just fine.

Tapestry of Tropic Temptations

Palm trees wave in dance,
Coconuts drop, more than chance.
Sipping drinks with tiny straws,
Laughter echoes, without pause.

Sandy toes in sun-warmed bliss,
Someone's hat gone, better miss!
Flip-flops slapping down the lane,
Chasing crabs, it's not in vain.

Cocktails spill on vibrant shirts,
As we dodge the sassy spurts.
Tropical birds with cheeky tones,
Stealing snacks from clumsy bones.

Under the sun's great parade,
Dance like no one's been invaded.
With each giggle, joy aligns,
In this wild, warm circus shines.

Dance of the Morning Mists

Waking up to vibrant light,
Misty dreams take playful flight.
Roosters crow with morning cheer,
While the coffee's brewing here.

Fog rolls slow like a dancer's twirl,
Bouncing through the coconut swirl.
Birds in matching feathered suits,
Sometimes sing, but often hoot!

Waves come crashing, with a grin,
As the fish splash, diving in.
Sunlight sparkles on the bay,
While beach balls bounce and sway.

A hammock calls with a gentle sway,
Where sun and giggles hold their play.
In this land of laughing bliss,
Who needs plans? Just take a kiss!

Voice of the Lapping Waves

Waves whisper secrets in the sand,
Tickling toes, making life grand.
Seashells giggle, hiding small,
Who put you up against the wall?

Flip-flops flapping with delight,
Chasing shadows, out of sight.
Children squeal as seagulls dive,
In this place, we feel alive.

Tide pools pop with slippery fun,
Crabby faces in the sun.
Laughter lingers on the breeze,
As we sway like palm tree leaves.

Splashing water, fresh and bright,
Echoes laughing, pure delight.
Salt-kissed air, we play and roam,
In this dream, we find our home.

The Soul of the Island Journey

Sunset paints the sky in hues,
While I dance in golden shoes.
A map of laughter in my hand,
Leading me to this bright land.

Drifting scents of spicy foods,
Curly hair, and jolly moods.
Every corner calls my name,
In this wild, delightful game.

Glimmering stars soon will rise,
Winking down from velvet skies.
Stories shared, with joy to glean,
Underneath the moon's soft sheen.

Between the trees, the night will hum,
A melody of bliss to come.
With each venturous step I take,
The island's heart, I soon will wake.

The Allure of Islands Unseen

On sandy shores where coconuts sway,
A crab in a tuxedo steals my chips away.
Seagulls squawk, as if taking a stand,
While I dance with my drink in a clumsy hand.

The waves giggle, whispering secrets untold,
To a sunburned tourist, so brave, yet so bold.
I chase a rogue wave, it slips from my grip,
Only to find seaweed's the real trip!

Memories Etched in Seashells

A shell in my pocket, a treasure I claim,
Each one has a story, or at least a name.
Like 'Gary the gorgeous' or 'Sandy the shy,'
They laugh as I wobble and trip on the fry.

The tide pulls and pushes with playful intent,
As crabs hold a meeting, in suits well-spent.
I join their confab, though confused by their ways,
They scuttle away, just a phase of my days.

Dreams Spread Like Wings in Serene Skies

Kites swirl and dip, like thoughts in my head,
But often they tangle, a colorful thread.
I reach for a dream, but it floats with the breeze,
Turning my hair into tropical cheese!

Flamingos parade, decked in pink sensational,
While I play hide and seek with a nuptial crab sensational.

Laughter erupts from a magical place,
As I find my lost flip-flop, stuck on a vase!

Harmonies Found Amongst Exotic Bloom

A flowered tune with a buzzing refrain,
The bees throw a party, but bring lots of pain.
I tiptoe around, wearing colors so bright,
And carefully dodge the bee's late-night flight.

In gardens of laughter, every petal's a jest,
As lizards join in, wearing tiny vests.
They dance on the walls, claiming this is their show,
While I munch on a mango, taking things slow.

Tranquility Tucked in Quiet Cove

In a cove where coconuts play,
The crabs dance in a funny way.
A parrot squawks, 'Don't bother me!'
While I sip my drink, so carefree.

The sun shines bright, oh what a sight,
But I forgot to sunscreen right.
Now I'm a lobster in disguise,
With rosy cheeks and squinty eyes.

A turtle jogs, what a slow pace,
I ask, 'Are you going to a race?'
He laughs and says, 'I take my time,
Life's a beach, and I'm in my prime!'

The waves whisper tales, soft and sweet,
But my flip-flops are missing their feet!
They've gone off to dance with the tide,
In this cove, joy and laughter abide.

Pathways through Vibrant Wilderness

Through jungles thick, I stumble around,
Losing my way without a sound.
A monkey swings by, gives me a grin,
Says, 'Follow me, let's see where you've been!'

The vines wave hello as I try to pass,
One wraps my ankle, oh what a laugh!
In a tangle, I dance, like a silly fool,
The jungle's my stage, and I'm breaking the rule.

Cicadas chirp their buzzing song,
But I can't tell if they're right or wrong.
A toucan claims it's all in the flair,
'Just join the rhythm, you'll learn how to share!'

Paths wind like noodles, twist and twine,
I declare, 'This jungle is truly divine!'
But just then I trip, what a glad surprise,
I land in the shade, with a grin on my eyes!

Secrets Unveiled by Mango Trees

Under trees where mangoes sway,
I found a lizard trying to play.
He says, 'Come join me, don't be shy!'
So I attempted, oh my, oh my!

The mangoes ripe, all golden and sweet,
But they're higher up—oh what a feat!
Jump and stretch, I miss by a mile,
The lizard just chuckles, in his green style.

I hear a giggle from a monkey nearby,
'You think you're the champ? Just give it a try!'
With gleeful hops, I aim for my goal,
Landing face-first, but it's part of the whole!

With mango juice dripping, I'm stuck in a smear,
But laughter erupts, oh, never fear!
In a sticky mess, my spirit's so free,
With the mangoes and laughter, just me and my glee!

Serenade of the Singing Sands

The grains all chatter, oh what a show,
They whisper secrets in a sunlit glow.
A seagull squawks, oh what a fuss,
It tries to steal the words from us.

With every step, the sands complain,
"Just lighten up, it's only pain!"
Flip-flops bouncing, like a mad ballet,
As laughter dances on the beach all day.

The barrels roll, the beach balls fly,
While silly hats tip off to the sky.
A crab joins in, with a sideways glance,
Declaring itself the king of the dance.

So here we are, with hair like hay,
A singalong to end the day.
The ocean's heart beats to our tune,
Life's a carnival, beneath the moon.

Dance of the Fireflies at Dusk

Blinking lights in the twilight air,
Fireflies flicker, with none a care.
They waltz and twirl in the warm night breeze,
As if they're casting spells with such ease.

An owl hoots, thinking it's wise,
But those little bugs, they steal the prize.
Zipping and zooming, they craft their flight,
While frogs just croak, trying to unite.

They swirl around like tiny stars,
While crickets chirp in raucous bars.
A glow worm dabs on some bright makeup,
And we all giggle at the ridiculous gaps.

So chase the lights, don't be shy,
The twinkling dance will never die.
Under the laughter and glittering charm,
The night winks, keeping us warm.

Tides of Time and the Endless Horizon

The waves might surf with a sassy grin,
They inch on shore, "Come join the win!"
A jellyfish floats with a pompous flair,
Like it won the contest for best in air.

Sandcastles rise, only to fall,
As the tide giggles, "You won't last at all!"
With a tiny flag, we claim our domain,
Just to watch it wash away again.

Seashells gather, a crafty crew,
Gossiping tales of the great fish stew.
A dolphin jumps, tries to take a bow,
While everyone shouts, "Just make it now!"

The horizon stretches, an open stage,
Each salty breeze, a turning page.
We're the jokers, with a pirate's jest,
Forever lost in the ocean's fest.

Harmony in the Heart of Paradise

In the jungle, the parrots squawk,
With silly outfits, they love to gawk.
Bananas peel in a twisty race,
While monkeys swing with a cheeky grace.

A toucan's beak, enormous and bright,
Acts as a mirror, reflecting our plight.
"Look at us," says a sloth, quite slow,
"Living life like a cozy show!"

The cicadas sing, a chorus loud,
While palm trees wiggle, oh so proud.
A turtle shuffles to the merry beat,
With a shell that's busier than your street.

So gather 'round for a giggling feast,\nWith fruit on the side, it's a nature's beast.
In this paradise, with laughter we weave,
A silly dream, in which we all believe.

Stories Carried on the Trade Winds

Funny tales ride the breezy air,
As parrots gossip without a care.
A crab in shorts, a hat on his head,
Wants to dance, but he trips instead.

Coconuts laugh, they roll and play,
Comedians in shells, both night and day.
The fish do flips, oh what a show,
Even the seaweed sways to and fro.

A flamingo with style, in shades so bright,
Sips on a drink, what a silly sight!
Turtles tell jokes that are quite absurd,
As waves carry laughter, all unheard.

Seagulls join in, with squawks and tweets,
A chorus of chuckles, oh look at their feats!
So take a moment and watch them thrive,
In this quirky realm where the wild ones jive.

Nightfall's Embrace in a Coastal Haven

Stars twinkle like fireflies in disguise,
As a crab sings karaoke, much to our surprise.
The fireflies gather for a dance on the shore,
While the moon rolls its eyes, 'Not this once more!'

A parrot in pajamas, so cozy and neat,
Complains 'I'm too tired' as he flaps his feet.
The beach blanket whispers, 'Hey, take a break!',
While sandcastles chuckle, 'What a mistake!'

A turtle in shades, cruising so slow,
Cracks up the crowd with his well-timed show.
The tide starts to tickle each creature around,
While laughter erupts, it's a comical sound.

The night slips away with giggle and sigh,
As the coastal haven waves a high goodbye.
So here's to the fun that the night gently brings,
In this paradise where the humor just sings.

Steps Through Lush Green Enchantment

With every step, the leaves burst in cheer,
As monkeys throw parties, my dear oh dear!
A sloth on a vine, moving quite slow,
Winks at the owl, 'Is this how you go?'

Lizards in tuxedos, all formal and spry,
Debate where to sunbathe or simply fly high.
The flowers start gossiping, petals aflutter,
While the breeze adds in, with a playful utter.

Ants conga line to a rhythm so sweet,
While frogs jump around, all tapping their feet.
A squirrel takes charge, conducting the fun,
As the whole forest savors the sun.

So wander through magic where humor is bright,
In this green wonderland, full of delight.
Every creature's a character, funny and bold,
In this enchanted world where stories unfold.

Swaying Rhythms of the Evening Tide

The waves dance lightly, a rhythmic embrace,
A clam flips a fin, oh, what a goofy grace!
Seashells wear sunglasses, playing it cool,
While octopuses giggle, showing their school.

Dolphins do tricks, sliding through the blue,
While a lazy sea lion waves just to you.
The tide brings in treasures both shiny and odd,
As crabs take a bow, feeling quite applauded.

A starfish in sneakers leads a conga line,
As jellyfish giggle, feeling divine.
The evening tide sways, making all feel alive,
In this seaside party, oh how we thrive!

So dance with the waves and sing to the night,
For the ocean's a stage, filled with sheer delight.
With laughter and joy, we are sure to abide,
In these swaying rhythms where fun cannot hide.

The Silent Song of the Mangrove

In the swamp where the crabs dance,
The trees whisper secrets at a glance.
Fish wear hats made of seaweed fine,
While frogs recite poems, sipping brine.

The air is thick, full of laughter light,
As dragonflies zoom, oh what a sight!
A crab tries to walk in a boogie way,
But slips on a leaf and shouts, "No way!"

A Canvas of Sunset Reflections

The sun dips low, orange and bright,
Painting the clouds with pure delight.
Parrots practice their evening chirp,
While lazy lizards take a nice burp.

A fisherman's hat flies off with glee,
Chased by a breeze, how funny to see!
He laughs and shouts, 'Hey, come back here!'
While the tidal waves roll, without any fear.

Delicate Petals and Salted Air

Flowers sway, dressed in colors bold,
While a bee buzzes tales yet untold.
The waves clap hands along the shore,
As seagulls argue, who's keeping score?

A kid builds castles with sand and cheer,
But a wave rolls in, it squeals, 'Oh dear!'
With a splash and a laugh, they both retreat,
And saltwater fish chuckle, is that a treat?

Celestial Wonders over Vibrant Canopies

Stars pop out 'neath the leafy crown,
While monkeys swing in their nightgown.
A sloth gives a wink, taking his time,
Swaying along to a whimsical rhyme.

A comet zips past, causing a stir,
As owls hoot loud, 'Did you see her blur?'
The night is filled with giggles and glee,
Under this starry jungle jubilee!

Voices of the Cucuruchos

In hats that tower, they march in glee,
With cucuruchos, they spill their tea.
Chasing chickens, they run and shout,
Grinning widely, there's no doubt.

With fanfare loud, the parade rolls on,
One trips and falls, the crowd laughs on.
A dance-off starts, oh what a sight,
With moves that surely take flight!

The crowd erupts, they cheer and laugh,
As someone spills their fizzy craft.
Cucuruchos spin like dizzy tops,
In wacky capers, the fun never stops!

From poppin' jokes to spilling snacks,
These lively folks have no relax.
Across the street, they joke and tease,
Life's a carnival in the tropical breeze!

Glimpse of Light through Palm Fronds

Sunlight dances through the leaves,
Where tiny critters pull their pranks, it believes.
A squirrel skitters, grabs a nut,
Then drops it down with a funny strut.

A bird takes flight, but not with grace,
It sticks the landing, round of space!
With tangled twigs stuck in its beak,
It fluffs its feathers, it's quite the geek!

A lizard lurks, its tongue flicks fast,
Watching the world in shades cast.
But when it jumps, oh what a sight,
It lands in a puddle with a splash and fright!

The sun sets low, it starts to gleam,
A chorus of giggles, like a dream.
Beneath the fronds, they laugh and play,
In this wacky land, it's another day!

Fusion of Sun and Sea

The sun slips down, the sea waves crash,
A surfboard tumbles, a hilarious splash.
With a goofy grin, a shark sings loud,
"I'm here to dance, come join the crowd!"

The crabs do hula, they've got some flare,
With tiny moves, they shimmy in the air.
A fish joins in, with fins a-waving,
The ocean floor is now misbehaving!

A beach ball bounces, a child's delight,
It flies off far, as dreams take flight.
A seagull swoops, it's got a plan,
To steal that ball – oh, what a scam!

Beneath the warmth, such laughter swells,
As sea turtles spin and everyone yells.
A fusion of fun, sun, and sea,
Where every wave brings out the glee!

Islands of Memory in the Ocean's Embrace

On sands so golden, memories bloom,
Where flip-flops race, and laughs consume.
A coconut falls with a thud and roll,
A picnic disaster, it steals the whole bowl!

Seagulls squawk, making friends with snacks,
While a tour guide fumbles with strange facts.
"Did you know turtles play beach ball too?"
The crowd bursts out, "Oh yes, they do!"

A hammock swings, caught in a breeze,
As someone naps, the island's tease.
But a mischievous monkey springs wide,
To steal sunglasses – what a wild ride!

From laughter's echo, sweet whispers flow,
In the ocean's embrace, they steal the show.
Islands of memory, with joy they trace,
A funny world, a warm-hearted place!

Ember Glow and Twilight's Kiss

As the sun dips low, the day starts to yawn,
A monkey on a branch dons a bathrobe and fawn.
Lizards play poker, they chuckle with glee,
While crickets hold concerts, just for the bee.

Coconuts drop with a serious thud,
The squirrel's mad dance turns into a dud.
Palm trees are swaying, they've had their three drinks,
With a wink from the moon, all the mischief thinks.

Nighttime descends with a wink and a sigh,
Fireflies are gossiping, oh my oh my!
The stars start to twinkle, and oh what a show,
But watch out for the owl, he's got quite the glow.

Laughter erupts with the breeze in a whirl,
Dancing around, even the colors will twirl.
So if you feel weary, just join in the fun,
Under the giggles of the moon and the sun.

Heartstrings of Chasing Shadows

In the garden of giggles, cactus wears shoes,
A flamingo's high kick will leave you bemused.
Underneath the sun, with a twirl and a spin,
The ants hold a parade, with a cheeky grin.

The shadows grow long, stretching over the sand,
A crab with a top hat gestures, quite grand.
Laughter carries on the wind like a kite,
As lizards do cha-chas, oh what a sight!

Bananas converse, sharing juicy old tales,
While the breeze, like a jester, tickles the sails.
Clouds wearing crowns march in a silly parade,
With a wink and a nudge, the atmosphere's played.

Take a leap in the party where silliness sings,
Shadows alive, wearing colorful wings.
In the heart of the night, with a cackle and cheer,
Let laughter be music, forever we'll steer.

Rich Earth and Azure Dreams

The mangoes are laughing, they're ripe and they're round,
While snails wear their shells, doing flips on the ground.
With fruit flies as guides, they dance in a line,
Around painted petals that twinkle and shine.

The earthworms get groovy, they boogie and sway,
While puddles hold mirrors, reflecting the play.
With colors so vibrant, the petals all scheme,
In the soil's rich embrace, we wake from a dream.

Coco palms perform ballet, graceful and spry,
And the sun takes a bow, saying bye-bye, oh my!
With every gust of wind, giggles bounce around,
As the playful spirits twirl into the ground.

So let's dance with the shadows and sing with the light,
Painting laugh lines in colors, both silly and bright.
In a world where the whimsy tickles our toes,
Plant your dreams in the laughter, watch how it grows.

Cradle of the Evening Tide

The ocean's a jester, with waves that can dance,
A starfish in glasses takes a moment to prance.
Seashells are gossiping, sharing old lore,
As dolphins in tuxedos create quite the score.

Beach balls are bouncing, telling jokes in the breeze,
While crabs wear their slippers, doing the squeeze.
Under the cover of a sky turning pink,
A conch shell is rapping, causing a wink.

Sandcastles giggle, they're quirky and bright,
With towers that wobble, and kings that take flight.
As the tide comes in softly, a foamy parade,
Each wave is a chuckle, in sunset's grand shade.

So gather your shadows and waltz with the tide,
Let the music of laughter be your evening guide.
In this cradle of silliness, we all will abide,
As the sea whispers secrets, from the moon far and wide.

Canvas of Colorful Sunsets

The sun paints skies with shades so bright,
Lemons and limes share in the light.
A coconut laughs, it rolls away,
While crabs do the cha-cha, come what may.

Palm trees sway, they dance so wild,
Sketching shadows, oh-so-styled.
A parrot yells, "Hey, get a tan!"
As tourists fish for the perfect plan.

A beach ball bounces, what a sight,
It lands on a sunbather, oh, what a fright!
Laughter erupts like the waves in June,
Sunset's a party, join in soon!

As colors swirl, the evening hums,
Even the seashells are humming drums.
With each brushstroke, a giggle drips,
In this realm, joy takes a few silly trips.

Soft Murmurs in Tropical Shadows

In the cool of shade, laughter floats,
Bananas wear hats, and mangoes gloat.
Palm fronds whisper secrets so light,
While iguanas ponder what's for bite.

Sunbathers snooze, their dreams take flight,
Chasing coconuts, they splash in delight.
A crab in sunglasses claims his throne,
Soft murmurs echo, it's party time, y'all!

Bright flip-flops dance, oh, what a flair,
While sea turtles giggle without a care.
The breeze carries tunes of a ukulele,
Mixing with laughter, so bright and cheery.

As shadows grow longer, the fun won't stop,
With pineapple drinks served in a chop.
In this paradise where silliness flows,
Every moment is a punchline, goodness knows.

Chill of the Trade Winds' Whisper

Chilly trade winds come for a dance,
They swirl around, asking for a chance.
A hammock swings, nearly in flight,
While tropical fish giggle, what a sight!

An octopus juggles with glee,
While beach chairs giggle, "Look at me!"
The waves share jokes from afar,
Even the sea turtles chuckle and spar.

Sunglasses wear the best of styles,
While crabs concoct hilarious wiles.
The sand tickles toes as it skips,
Clouds cruise overhead, making quips.

As the sun dips low, mischief brews,
Trade winds whisper shade, not the blues.
In this cool breeze, joy is unconfined,
Where laughter's the compass and fun is enshrined.

Secrets Written in the Sand

Footprints dance like they know the tune,
Secrets scribbled, oh-so-soon.
A starfish chuckles, plump and grand,
Eavesdropping on tales drawn in the sand.

A beachcomber found a shoe, oh dear,
Could it be left by a pirate, I fear?
Seashells giggle as the tide rolls by,
Stirring dreams of mermaids that sigh.

A crab tells jokes about sandy bumps,
While sunbathers snicker at the thumps.
The wind carries whispers of laughter sweet,
As waves compile stories at our feet.

In fleeting whispers, secrets unfold,
In grains of sand, treasures untold.
As the tide pulls back, waves burst with glee,
In every giggle lives a memory.

Soliloquy of the Southern Skies

A bird just landed, plump and round,
He stole my sandwich from the ground.
The sun's too bright, I squint and grin,
Who knew my lunch would be his win?

The palm trees sway, they dance and tease,
A lizard sips the gentle breeze.
I tripped on sand, fell like a star,
While crabs just watched from near and far.

The clouds parade in polka dots,
While fish wear hats, or so I thought.
A boat is stuck, the captain's mad,
But I just laugh; it's all I've had.

With sunscreen smeared like war paint thick,
Here comes my friend, with jokes to kick.
We'll laugh until the day is done,
In this wild, wacky, golden fun.

Murmurs of the Wandering Pelican

A pelican just stole my hat,
He flew away with quite a spat.
I chased him down, all flapping arms,
He laughed aloud, my fashion harms!

The tide rolled in, a cheeky wave,
Pulled footprints back, so rude, so brave.
My toes now squish in gooey muck,
The ocean's humor—what's my luck?

Nearby a turtle, wise and slow,
Said, 'Hey, take life nice and low!'
But I'm too busy dodging gulls,
Who aim for snacks, like playful bulls.

The sky's a circus, full of flight,
And I'm the clown—what a delight!
With laughter ringing, loud and clear,
I'll find my hat—not far, I fear.

The Essence of Tropical Whispers

Rumbling thunder made the flowers dance,
Just as the bugs began to prance.
The breeze brings whispers, oh so bold,
Of mischief brewing in the gold.

A monkey swings with carefree glee,
He's made my drink—how rude is he?
I watched him chug my coconut,
With careless style—what a nut!

The sky erupts with colors bright,
As crabs declare a dance-off night.
The waves applaud, the stars peek through,
While I'm stuck dancing in a stew!

The fireflies blink like little jokes,
As laughter mingles with the yolks.
With sunburned skin and wild delight,
The tropical giggles fill the night.

Butterflies in a Sunlit Reverie

Butterflies giggle on flowers' heads,
I join the fun, skipping my dreads.
A breeze whispers secrets, soft and sweet,
While ants assemble for a high-stakes meet.

I tried to chat with a busy bee,
But all I got was a stinger spree.
He buzzed away with a buzzing smart,
I waved goodbye, but it broke my heart.

The sun's a clown, it tosses rays,
Turning my lemonade into a blaze.
But laughter cools this sappy plight,
As I breakdance in the warm sunlight.

A parrot squawks, a tale from the past,
Oh, what a wild and colorful cast!
With giggles bright and playful quest,
This sunlit stage has its very best.

Footprints Under a Fiery Sky

A monkey stole my hat today,
Left me with a funky fray.
I chased him through the silver sand,
He laughed and danced, oh wasn't it grand?

A crab pinched my toe in glee,
Said, "You can't catch that monkey, see?"
With each step, my flip-flops flop,
As locals point and giggle nonstop.

A seagull swooped to say hello,
With a wink and a flirty show.
I offered him a chip or two,
He took them all, what a sneaky view!

As sun descends, the colors burst,
With every laugh, my heart's well-nursed.
So here I stand on this wild spree,
Footprints laughing in a sandy spree.

Stars Above the Island Canopy

The stars wink down with cheeky grace,
As I trip over my own shoelace.
One twinkled bright, shouted, "Look out!"
I stumbled, fell, and let out a shout!

The trees overhead sway and sway,
I think they laugh at my clumsy play.
A firefly buzzed around my ear,
"Catch me if you can!" it was clear.

A coconut dropped with a thud,
I swore it laughed, then rolled in the mud.
The night was bright, a perfect jest,
As I searched for my way, an uninvited guest.

Stars burst forth, a dazzling parade,
I danced with shadows, unafraid.
With each joyful slip and stumble bright,
Beneath the cosmic giggles of the night.

Blossoms Unfurled in the Warmth

In the garden, blooms come out to play,
Petals prancing in a silly display.
A bee said, "Watch me do my dance!"
I twirled with joy, took my chance!

The flowers giggle, colors in a fuss,
One asked, "Can you keep up with us?"
I puffed and laughed, my heart alive,
As buds laughed loud, I felt the thrive.

The sunbeams tickled every cheek,
While butterflies flapped, oh what a streak!
A snail crept by, slow as could be,
Said, "Why rush? Just enjoy the spree!"

As blossoms danced in the breezy light,
I joined the fun, what a delightful sight!
In the warmth of laughter and glee,
Nature's party was wild and free.

Melody of the Misty Morn

Misty morn brings a quirky tune,
Roosters crow in a goofy swoon.
As I trip over my pet's long tail,
The cat just smirks, without fail.

The ocean whispers with a bubbly cheer,
A wave pranked me, oh dear, oh dear!
I stumbled back, soaked to the core,
And laughed with the fish, wanting more.

A parrot perched, colors so bright,
Said, "Keep it up; it's quite a sight!"
Its laughter echoed through the trees,
As I joined in, feeling the breeze.

With every giggle that floats on high,
The day awakens under a lively sky.
In the misty glow, I dance along,
To the melody of the morning's song.

Mystical Tides and Melancholy Waves

Waves roll in with a splashy grin,
I thought I saw a fish wearing a fin.
The gulls are gossiping, oh what a sight,
As crabs dance jigs in the pale moonlight.

Seashells whisper secrets of the shore,
One's telling jokes; I can't take it anymore.
The tide laughs loud as it ebbs and flows,
While I try to catch those silly pink toes.

Has an octopus signed my beach ball's fate?
It tickles me silly; I feel quite great!
Mysterious tides, with their comical flair,
Bring giggles and chuckles to salty air.

So let's raise a toast to this goofy scene,
With a coconut drink and a frothy sheen.
For happiness oozes from every nook,
As fishy tales swirl like an old storybook.

Echoes of Laughter in the Palm Shadows

In the shade of palms, I hear a song,
Sung by lizards, oh, how they throng!
Their tiny tails twitch to the beat,
While I sit back, enjoying the heat.

Belly laughs float on the warm, sweet breeze,
As parrots squawk jokes, aiming to please.
A monkey swings by, with a grin so wide,
Snatching my hat; then it takes a ride!

Children chase shadows, their giggles abound,
While a turtle attempts to dance on the ground.
The island is lively, a raucous affair,
With fun-loving creatures that leap through the air.

As the sun dips low, the laughter stays bright,
Kites chase the twilight, all sparkling with light.
In this funny realm, joy forever flows,
With echoes of laughter in every breeze that blows.

Embrace of the Island Spirits

The spirits arise when the sun hits the shore,
In flip-flops they dance, who could ask for more?
With coconut drinks in their ghostly hands,
They jiggle and giggle across the soft sands.

I joined in the fun, just me and my hat,
But my dance was more wobble than graceful acrobat.
The spirits just chuckled; I tripped on a shell,
As they twirled and glided, I stumbled and fell.

With laughter they scooped me up from the ground,
In their bubbly embrace, joy clearly found.
They polished my dance moves, made them quite fab,
Now I am the talk of the palm tree slab!

With an arm over shoulder, we shimmied till dawn,
Adventures of laughter and coconut fronds.
For in this wild realm, spirits take flight,
In an embrace of pure mirth, under starlit night.

Wind's Serenade in Lush Green Valleys

The wind knows my name, it whispers with glee,
Twirling past flowers, it teases a bee.
With a whoosh and a swirl, it plays with my hair,
While I giggle at antics without a care.

Banana leaves clap to the wind's jazzy beat,
As fruit bats audition with flappy, fun feats.
The hills start to chuckle, they rumble and roll,
A wind symphony, igniting the soul.

I ran with the breeze, kicked up leaves in a whirl,
Chasing a butterfly, a soft, breezy twirl.
And the monkeys, oh my, they performed quite a show,
Swinging through trees, with the lightest of flow.

As the sun paints the valleys in hues bright as day,
The wind serenades us; forever we sway.
In this green paradise, joy wildly prevails,
And laughter still dances on sweet, gentle gales.

Philosophy of the Tide and Time

The wave said to the sand, "You're not my type,"
"I like to splish, while you just wipe!"
The crab danced sideways with a grin,
"Why worry about time, when the fun's in the spin?"

The sun just laughed, its rays a tease,
"Forget your worries, and ride the breeze!"
A fish jumped up, made quite a splash,
"I just found a shell, come on, let's dash!"

Seashells giggled in the sun's warm glow,
"You humans rush, we take it slow!"
Above, the seagulls sang a tune,
"Life's a party, come dance with the moon!"

So here they danced, in a jovial tide,
Through laughter and waves, they let joy glide.
In their world of fun, worries did fade,
A philosophy made, in sunshine displayed.

The Soliloquy of Stars Above

Stars whispered secrets in the night,
"We twinkle just to cause delight!"
The moon rolled by, a silver ball,
"Why so serious? Let's have a ball!"

Comets raced, with tails so bright,
"Catch us, catch us, in your night fright!"
While planets giggled, round and round,
"We're just here to spin and astound!"

A shooting star slipped, gave a wink,
"Wish away, live without a blink!"
The galaxy hummed a cosmic tune,
"Float your cares away, under the moon!"

So join the fun, let laughter soar,
The universe invites you to explore.
With every twinkle, a joke to share,
In the cosmos' jest, find joy everywhere!

Reflections in Crystal Blue Depths

In the water, fish grin wide,
"We swim in circles, come for a ride!"
A turtle snorted, dropping slow,
"Time's just a game, let the ocean flow!"

Seagrass swayed to the rhythm below,
"Dance with the waves, feel the flow!"
A dolphin jumped, all gleeful and bright,
"The ocean's a stage, let's put on a flight!"

Coral laughed in colors so bold,
"We tell tales, secrets unfold!"
A little shrimp chimed in with a spark,
"Who knew the sea could be this much a lark?"

So dive right in, let troubles drift,
In the crystal blue depths, find your gift.
With every splash, a chuckle revealed,
In the ocean's embrace, joy is sealed.

Whispers of the Island Breeze

The breeze giggled, tickling my face,
"Why walk when you can dance in this space?"
Leaves rustled softly, joining the song,
"Let's sway and swirl, you can't go wrong!"

Coconuts chuckled, hanging from trees,
"Life's a beach party, come catch the breeze!"
The sun blinked bright, with a wink so sly,
"Just lay back, let the good times fly!"

Crickets serenaded, a late-night show,
"Join us for laughter, let your worries go!"
A parrot squawked, with a joke so racy,
"Hanging with me? It's always spacey!"

So feel the joy, let your spirits lift,
With whispers and laughter, life's a gift.
In the island's embrace, fun never ends,
Where every moment is a song with friends.

The Laughter of Waves and Sunbeams

The waves giggle as they crash,
Their foamy hands make a splash.
Sunbeams dance like joyful sprites,
Tickling toes on summer nights.

A crab winks with a sideways glance,
While fish in bubbles twirl and prance.
Seashells chuckle on the shore,
As seagulls join the beach's roar.

Palm trees sway in playful jive,
Their leafy arms are all alive.
In this realm of salty cheer,
Life's a joke, I think, my dear.

So let us laugh, oh, what a sport,
With every wave, we laugh and snort.
The ocean's humor never ends,
In sunlit breezes, joy transcends.

Echoes of Paradise in a Starry Night

Stars twinkle like they're up to tricks,
Whispering secrets, short and quick.
Moonbeams play tag on the shore,
While crickets join in for a score.

In the stillness, coconuts tease,
Wobbling on their trunks with ease.
A nightingale croons a silly tune,
As fireflies blink like little moons.

Laughter drifts on the warm night air,
Bouncing off trees without a care.
The ocean giggles, a gentle wave,
As if to say, "Come on, be brave!"

In the heart of this starry embrace,
We find joy in this light-hearted place.
For even the night has its playful side,
Where echoes of fun and dream collide.

Conch Shell Secrets in the Moonlight

Conch shells hold tales of the sea,
Whispering secrets just for me.
At night they giggle under the stars,
Telling stories of drunk sea farers.

Moonlight dapples the sandy floor,
Where crabs do the cha-cha, evermore.
Shells blushing pink say, 'Listen near!'
You'll hear the waves cracking up, I hear.

A dolphin leaps with a splashy cheer,
Says, 'Why so serious? Have no fear!'
With every swirl, the tide confides,
Life's a joke where laughter abides.

So gather 'round and lend an ear,
To the conch's giggles, crystal clear.
For moonlit nights and shell-bound glee,
Bring forth the joy of wild decree.

Raindrops Playing on Thatched Roofs

Raindrops tap dance on the roof,
A rhythm that makes the heart go woof!
Each plink and plop carries a tune,
Singing songs to the lazy afternoon.

Thatched roofs laugh with a gentle sway,
As puddles form in a playful array.
The breeze joins in with a silly swoop,
While frogs croak like they're in a troupe.

Colors splash as the clouds bestow,
A watercolor show from nature's throw.
The raindrops giggle, slipping past,
A playful storm that never lasts.

So let the rain sing out its cheer,
While we twirl and spin without a fear.
For in this wild, watery delight,
Laughter blooms in the softest night.

Celestial Canvas of Endless Light

The sun wears shades and makes a show,
Clouds dance around in a breezy flow.
A seagull squawks, thinking it's a star,
Chasing its shadow, flying afar.

Lemons roll down from the palm tree's crown,
As laughter bubbles up from the town.
A kid on a surfboard, looks like a pro,
But face-plants right in, oh what a show!

Pineapples strut with sunglasses on,
While coconuts giggle until they're gone.
Bikinis twirl in the golden heat,
As beach balls bounce in a rhythmic beat.

Under this canopy of vibrant cheer,
Even the grumps can't help but jeer.
In this land of whimsy, cheeky and bright,
Every day feels like a pure delight.

Cage of the Morning's Embrace

Roosters shout like they own the day,
While sleepyheads groan, just wanting to stay.
Coffee brews loud, like a rock band in tune,
While toast pops up, just a little too soon.

Flip-flops squeak with each silly step,
A crab waves high, oh what a prep!
The sun throws confetti across the ground,
And laughter escapes as joy spins around.

Fried eggs take flight, doing the slide,
As breakfast becomes an unplanned ride.
Bananas decide to launch a parade,
While syrupy giggles start to cascade.

In the cage of joy, we're forever young,
With playful hearts, we're all bit unsung.
Each morning holds a merry embrace,
In this quirky, sun-kissed, lively space.

Twilight's Palette of Soft Hues

As the sun dips low with a wink and grin,
Crickets begin their mischievous din.
Cotton candy skies turn a shade of fun,
While fireflies gather for a sparkling run.

Beach towels now become the dance floor,
Bumping and laughing, who could ask for more?
A crab brings chips, feeling quite sly,
While mermaids giggle as bubbles fly.

Shadows stretch like taffy on sand,
As the moon tosses glitter across the land.
Kids chase the glow, daring each other,
Pretending to be as light as a feather.

In the sunset's joy, all worries cease,
With sandy feet, our hearts find peace.
Under this whimsical twilight show,
Every laugh echoes wherever we go.

The Spirit of the Severed Seas

Waves tumble like puppies on the shore,
Catching bright shells, who could ask for more?
A fish in a hat gives a wink and a wave,
While dolphins plot the next big rave.

The octopus juggles with flair and grace,
While crabs on the sand dance a silly race.
Seagulls steal snacks with a cheeky sip,
While flip-flops trip, what a hilarious slip!

Bubbles float up in a giggling spree,
Whispers of seaweed join in the glee.
The tide rolls in, it is party time,
With laughter and waves in perfect rhyme.

In this spirit that's free as the breeze,
Every splash brings a moment to seize.
With shimmering joy in a salty embrace,
Life takes on a whimsical trace.

Journey Through the Tropical Tides

Waves like giggles, splashing high,
A crab in sneakers scurries by.
Sunbathers grin, they tease the breeze,
While seagulls steal their tasty peas.

The sand's a blanket, sticky sweet,
With ice cream cones that tumble neat.
A dolphin winks, a cheeky prank,
As surfers fall — oh, what a clank!

Palm trees sway in curious dance,
As tourists trip in sunlit chance.
With coconut hats and mismatched socks,
They pose with parrots and forget their clocks.

Kisses from a Warm Horizon

The sunset paints a silly grin,
As ducks play hopscotch on the skin.
A pineapple samba by the shore,
While beach balls bounce and crashing roars.

Chasing surfboards, dodging sand,
A sunburned fool won't understand.
He slips and slides with a joyful yell,
As laughter rings like a fruity bell.

Flip-flops flapping, toes exposed,
With tan lines drawn in funny codes.
Seashells whisper ancient jokes,
To beachgoers clad in matchless cloaks.

Serenity Overlooked by Feathered Friends

A parrot squawks a saucy line,
As toucans toast with fruity wine.
They Chatter 'neath a leafy spree,
While humans join in quirky glee.

A sloth on a branch, stuck in thought,
Dreams of tacos — that's the plot!
While monkeys swing in silly haste,
A picnic goes to feathered taste.

With nature's noise, a merry song,
As butterfly parties float along.
Each flutter brings a laugh, a cheer,
In the canopy, joy is clear.

Enchantment in the Afternoon Light

Sun-kissed moments, laughter's glow,
As hammocks sway and breezes flow.
A squirrel juggles with a nut,
While tourists try to dance, but — what?

Vintage shades on cheeky faces,
As flip-flops win the fashion races.
Splashing puddles, kids in delight,
The ocean giggles, invites a fight.

At sunset's blush, they toast a plan,
With juice-filled cups and sunburned skin.
In the twilight, shadows twist and twine,
With memories brewed like fancy wine.

Footprints in the Tropics

In flip-flops I strut, with a style so grand,
Each footprint I leave, looks like I planned.
But crabs on the shore, they mimic my walk,
With sideways moves, they mock and they talk.

A parrot squawks loud, "Why don't you try?"
I slipped on some sand, oh me, oh my!
The sun gives a wink, as I tumble around,
The laughter of waves is a whimsical sound.

I danced with a palm tree, we twirled in the breeze,
It laughed and it swayed, oh how it could tease!
As coconuts drop with a thud on my head,
I crack up and chuckle, my humor widespread.

So here in this place, where the sun never sets,
I tumble and giggle, no room for regrets.
With each little misstep, I find pure delight,
In the funny footprints of my tropical flight.

A Symphony of Colors in Bloom

Flowers dance brightly, in pinks and in yellows,
They sway with the breeze, such cheerful little fellows.
Bees zoom and they buzz, in a flurry of glee,
Can you hear them all sing? Well, maybe not me!

There's a rose with a frown, just won't lift its head,
"Too bright!" it insists, "I'd rather stay red!"
But daisies all giggle, "Come join the parade!"
And the violets whisper, "Don't hide, be afraid!"

The sun throws its rays, like a spotlight on show,
But some leaves turn brown, in the tropical glow.
"I thought we were green!" they all grumble and pout,
As the rainbow looks on, then it starts to shout.

With laughter in petals, the garden's alive,
"Let's share all our colors, and give them a jive!"
So, join the brigade, in this floral delight,
Where colors unite and all bloom with pure light.

Secrets of the Jungle at Dusk

The jungle is buzzing, as night starts to creep,
A sloth starts a rumor, while pandas just sleep.
Monkeys are laughing, swinging from trees,
While a gecko in shades claims it's quite the tease!

A toucan with style struts on a branch,
"Look at my beak, doesn't it enhance?"
But the owls just hoot, "What a curious sight!"
While fireflies twinkle, they flare up the night.

A snake tells a tale, slithering with glee,
"Once I was handsome, a sight, you would see!"
But the frogs just croak, with a ribbiting cheer,
"Your charm still remains, oh friend, have no fear!"

In the twilight's embrace, the jungle is wild,
With nature's own laughs, it's a joy to be riled.
Secrets and giggles swirl all around,
Where everything's funny, and smiles abound.

Where the Ocean Meets the Horizon

The ocean waves crash, they laugh with a splash,
As I build a grand castle, a work of pure trash.
The tide pulls it down, oh, what a big joke!
With seaweed for moats, it's more magic than smoke!

Seagulls dive down, they steal all my fries,
With a squawk and a flap, they've got sly little eyes.
"Oh come back!" I yell, "Those are mine!" they just scream,
As I wave my hands wildly, I'm lost in a dream!

The sun winks at me, wearing a golden hue,
While sand gets between every toe, oh boo-hoo!
But laughter is here and the joy's on a roll,
As I dance with the waves, let the sea take its toll!

So here on the edge, where horizons extend,
Each giggle's a treasure, and each wave is a friend.
As the sun starts to set, painting skies all aglow,
The dance of the ocean is the best comedy show!

The Call of the Coral Reef

In the splash of a fish, I lose my cool,
A clown with a grin, he jumps in the pool.
The seaweed's a dance, a shimmy and sway,
While starfish just lounge, enjoying the day.

The dolphins all giggle, they leap in delight,
Jellyfish float by, looking quite light.
The octopus juggles, with tentacles spread,
While the seahorses gossip, all filled with dread.

A crab with no care scuttles by for a snack,
He's wearing a shell, not the fashion to lack.
The coral is blushing, a rainbow so bright,
While fish dress in stripes; oh, what a sight!

So come take a dive, in the fun and the cheer,
With laughter and bubbles, there's nothing to fear.
For under the waves, where the whims take flight,
Life's one big party, from morning to night.

Sanctuary of the Silken Waves

The waves in their gowns dance a silky affair,
While sea turtles waltz, rather debonair.
A crab struts his stuff, all fancy and suave,
While sea cucumbers just silently carve.

The pelicans glide, with a wink and a tease,
They dive for a snack, with elegant ease.
A flamingo tries yoga, but loses his pose,
With a splosh of pastel, he's quite the doze.

As sandcastles rise with great glee and with glee,
The tide steals a piece, as if playing a spree.
Seagulls are squawking, a raucous, loud choir,
While shells play the drums, with a beat to inspire.

So don your best shades, and lay on your towel,
For in the bright sun, the whole world will scowl.
At the foolishness found in the waves and the sand,
Where silly adventures are forever unplanned.

Twilight's Embrace on Island Sands

As the sun takes a bow, in colors so rare,
The lizards all gather, with nothing to wear.
A coconut falls, with a thud on the floor,
While crickets play tunes, a sweet island score.

The palm trees all sway, like they're lost in a dream,
While fireflies twinkle, the night's sparkling gleam.
A frog leaps around, on a quest for a friend,
With more hops than sense, it's a laugh without end.

A toucan shows off, with a beak full of flair,
He dances with rhythm, in the warm evening air.
While the moon sings its lullaby, soft and light,
The stars twirl above, in a festive delight.

So sip on your drink, with an umbrella in sight,
As the island's sweet magic enchants the night.
In this realm of the goofy, the fun never ends,
Where joy is a language, and all are true friends.

Heartbeats of the Rainforest

In the jungle so lush, where the wild parrots squawk,
A monkey swings by, with a fashionable walk.
The sloths are just chilling, hanging out on a tree,
While toucans debate, sippin' nectar with glee.

The frogs are a chorus, with tunes so absurd,
Their jumps cause a ruckus, each note quite unheard.
A snake in a hat, claims a throne made of leaves,
While chattering squirrels play dress-up in sleeves.

The jaguar ponders, with a grin on his face,
"Why chase when I nap? That's my favorite place!"
While the butterflies giggle, in colors so bold,
They flutter like letters, with stories untold.

So let's dance in the rain, twirling leaf and twig,
In a world full of smiles, where nothing's too big.
For in these wild heartbeats, laughter is found,
In the rainforest magic, all joy knows no bound.

Kisses from the Ocean Breeze

The sea whispers secrets, oh what a tease,
A wave rolls in, planting kisses with ease.
I jumped, and I slipped, straight into the foam,
Now I'm the mermaid of my own silly home.

With seagulls laughing, they call out my name,
I shout back in glee, and they join in the game.
Saltwater tangles my hair in a mess,
Laughter erupts as I fashion a dress.

The surfboards all giggle, stacked high on the sand,
The sun-drenched day, clutching winks from the land.
As crabs juggle snacks, flipping shells with a cheer,
My troubles fly away, they just disappear.

Breezes tickle toes; it's best not to fight,
Each gust brings a chuckle, full of delight.
So join in the laughter, come take a spin,
Let those kisses from the ocean begin!

Fragrance of Passionflower Dreams

In a garden of giggles, the flowers all dance,
Passionfruit whispers, they're giving romance.
Bees buzz by wearing their fancy bow ties,
While butterflies flit, sharing gossip and lies.

The scent of weird blooms makes noses go wild,
I snort and I sneeze, like a baffled child.
With petals like pillows all fluffing the air,
I trip on a vine; oh, you wouldn't dare!

Daisies are laughing, they poke at my toes,
Who knew that the garden had such funny woes?
The fruits roll like barrels, all juicy and fine,
In this fragrant circus, oh, how we all shine!

Dreams drift through petals, causing some ruckus,
As the perfumes of passion entice all the fuss.
So let's twirl and giggle beneath leafy streams,
In the heartbeat of flowers, embrace silly dreams!

Dusk Descends on Paradise Shores

As the sun drops low, painting skies with delight,
The crickets strike up with a tune for the night.
Dancing in shadows, with mischief they prance,
Bats swoop around like they're sporting new pants.

The moon winks at lizards, they laugh in surprise,
A clam shells out jokes, he's quite the wise guy.
Coconut palms sway, doing silly old moves,
While the stars twinkle down, as if joining grooves.

The surf sips the shore, in a bubbly farewell,
Where mermaids tell tales, and the dolphins all yell.
Nightfall is silly; with capers galore,
As dinosaurs dance on the tropical shore!

So toast to the dusk; let your worries take flight,
The funny side wins on this magical night.
With laughter as currency under moonbeam light,
We'll giggle and smile till the morning feels bright!

The Color of Coconut Lullabies

Lullabies whispered from hushed, swaying trees,
Coconuts chuckle as they float in the breeze.
A parrot takes flight, with a wink and a squawk,
Singing sweet nonsense, as if it could talk.

Crabs in tuxedos chatting under the stars,
Regale with tales of their famous bazaar.
As shells clap their hands to the rhythm of night,
The ocean hums softly, a melody bright.

In the warmth of the moon, the coconuts grin,
They sway to the tunes, and the laughter creeps in.
Jump in the sand, for a dance with a twist,
Catch a coconut drop—it's an impossible list!

So join in the revels, with each bouncy note,
Where dreams in the color of coconuts float.
As slumber sets sail on this whimsical ride,
Come snuggle with nonsense; let joy be your guide!

Spirits of the Sunlit Jungle

Monkeys dance with a silly grin,
Parrots joke about where to begin.
Lizards lounge in the golden light,
Chasing shadows left and right.

The sloths hang low, take their sweet time,
While jaguars groan, saying, "Oh, sublime!"
Coconuts drop like comical bombs,
Who knew jungle life could have such charms?

The toucans wear hats, oh what a sight,
Swapping gossip 'til the fall of night.
With every giggle, the trees seem to sway,
In this crazy jungle, we laugh all day!

A frog croaks a tune, so off-key,
Yet all the critters still hum with glee.
So let's toast to laughter in vibrant shades,
In this sunlit jungle, fun never fades!

Echoes of the Ocean's Heart

Waves giggle softly, an echoing cheer,
While crabs in tuxedos wander near.
Fish fashion shows, shimmering bright,
Sardines cause a splash! What a sight!

Starfish in tutus twirl on the sand,
While clams hold a talent show, how grand!
Seagulls squawk out their best one-liners,
As dolphins playdate becomes all the finer.

A hermit crab sneezes, causing a splash,
With a dash and a swirl, it's quite the clash!
Ocean creatures, laugh until it's dark,
Painting the sea with their joyful spark.

As the sun dips low, the laughter can't fade,
In the heart of the sea, all memories are made.
So let's surf on giggles and ride the tide,
In this comical ocean, come take a slide!

Dreams of a Caribbean Twilight

Twilight dances on the waves' edge,
Coconuts fall—Ouch! What a hedge!
The palm trees whisper, "Time for fun!"
As the light fades, the laughter's begun.

Crickets chirp jokes, a witty ensemble,
While fireflies join in—a sparkling jumble.
The moon, a clown, inflates with style,
Painting the night with a mischievous smile.

A salsa party on the sandy shore,
With conga lines that shake and roar.
Mermaids giggle, their tails a swirl,
In this twilight, dreams are a whirl.

So bring out the rum, let the calypso play,
As the stars wink down, let's dance all day.
In the Caribbean vibe, laughter's the key,
Where every sunset inspires such glee!

Kaleidoscope of Exotic Blooms

Flowers wear skirts, twirling on their stems,
Bumbling bumblebees play hide and gem.
Petals gossip, they whisper and cheer,
While butterflies flutter, spreading good cheer.

A cactus cracks jokes, clever and spry,
While daisies giggle, they can't help but sigh.
Hibiscus host a swaying parade,
With a colorful flair that can't be delayed.

Orchids grumble about their tea time,
As violets blend in with the lime.
In this blooming chaos, laughter's a breeze,
As the sun's warm glow aims to please.

So let's dance in the garden, freeze-frame delight,
In this kaleidoscope world, everything's bright.
With sprightly blooms and flamboyant glee,
Nature's funny, come join the spree!

www.ingramcontent.com/pod-product-compliance
Lightning Source LLC
Chambersburg PA
CBHW072219070526
44585CB00015B/1404